intertwined

celina maeve

embrace the
boundless power
of self-love

claim your free, exclusive 2-week
self-love workbook at:

celinamaeve.com

work on your relationship...with *yourself*

14 days of exercises to help you love
yourself--just as you are!

unraveling

1

untangling

49

tying

106

unraveling

unconditional love
is not
romantic

if you love someone
without conditions
they can treat you horribly
do whatever they want to you
and expect you to still love them
no matter what

if you love someone
who doesn't treat you well
you are giving them
all the love
that is supposed to be
for yourself

-conditions are boundaries

in the beginning
we lit each other up
one laugh
one touch
one look
we were bright
we were dazzling
we were the sun
every morning noon and night

after a while
we were a cozy fire
less sizzle, more warmth
the kind that evicts the chill
from your bones
a dimmer light
but one that suited us
just right

now i have to light
my own flames
passion and purpose
fun and games
but none of the sparks
come from you

     -dimming

you say
your love language
is physical touch

so why
won't you touch me
the way i want

imagine
if *i*
did that to *you*

you'd be out the door
getting it
from someone else

somehow you're always
the one
who's properly satisfied

so relaxed you fall asleep
leaving me
unfinished

frustrated
needs unmet
desires unfulfilled

if physical touch
is your love language

you don't love me

you love yourself

-you're finished

when he texts you
feel better
but goes out with his friends
he's showing you
where your wellbeing
falls on his list
of priorities

-listen to his actions, not his words

my heart
doesn't understand
why you ~~can't~~
~~don't~~
choose not to
put in the same effort
as i do

-i don't feel the love

if you have to ask
if he's trying

he's not.

-neglect is hideous once you see it

i refuse
to make
my emotions
smaller
to make you
more comfortable
any longer

i deserve my anger
my sadness
my pain

i deserve my frustration
filling up the room
and your eardrums

i'm not a bitch
i'm a human
who is tired
of managing
your emotions
and reactions
simply because you can't

—taking up emotional space

i put all my energy
into caring for you
forgetting to leave any
for myself
but you
were only putting
minimal energy
into caring for me

no wonder you were shocked
when i said it wasn't working

your cup was overflowing
with my love and your own
but mine only had a few drops
scattered at the bottom

-running on empty

if you're just fine
with me
doing more
caring more
loving more
than you,
we don't have
a true partnership

that is not my idea
of a real relationship

-partners?

you broke me
slowly
like the ocean
turning glass
into sand

i didn't notice
you sanding off
tiny fragments
of my heart
until i had to scoop
what remained
into a bucket
with a shovel

-sand

the feelings of others
are not my burdens
to carry
or protect
or tip-toe around
just like my feelings
are not a burden
for others to carry

-regulate only your own feelings

when someone
tells you
your dreams
are too
big

don't
believe
them

  -dream on

~~you broke my heart~~
~~i broke my heart~~
~~we broke my heart~~

you and i both
broke my heart

separately.

we chipped away at it slowly
like sculptors
with chisels
made of words
and thoughts
and
silence.

but instead of a beautiful
masterpiece
we were left with a messy pile of rubble
that you got to walk away from
unscathed

the mess was me
and like most messes
it had to get worse
before it could get better

even though you broke it
i knew you wouldn't fix it
but i broke it too
so fix it i will do

–whoever breaks it must fix it

if another woman
can "steal" him from you
he was never really yours

-and that's his fault

i know
it is not my fault
but here i am
blaming myself
again

-*toxic thoughts*

you've made me question
every. single. thing.
about our relationship

the world is so cold
how does anyone
have the willpower
to leave their warm blankets
knowing what awaits them
they must be so brave

-courageous against the cold

our capacity
for pain
is immense
perhaps limitless

                    it is the cost we pay
              for our immense capacity
                              for love

              -we can love deeply because we can
              hurt deeply

this is just a rough patch, right?
any day now you're going to
burst in the door
and profess how sorry you are
explain that it was the biggest mistake
you've ever made
that you've learned your lesson
that we're meant to be together
that you'll make it up to me
and it'll never happen again

...right?

we were supposed to be together
for exactly forever
i know how your voice sounds
when you first wake up
you know how i look without make-up
we shared hopes and dreams
and beds and drinks
actually, we shared everything
you've touched every single
square inch of me
i thought you were my
one true love story
our lives were so beautifully entangled
now they just look ugly and mangled

-intimate ~~forever~~ never again

what if i was never enough for you?
what if i was just convenient?
what if you never loved me?
what if you just said you loved me
to collect the benefits of my affections?

-my fears about us after we ended

heartbreak is a haunting mist
shrouding the heart
blanketing its chambers
dampening its beats
weighing it down
casting a veil of sadness
obscuring all clarity
enveloping the spirit
in a haze of regretful longing

right now
i think i would give up
a future love story
of mine
just to relive ours

i don't want someone else
i want you

depression is a sneaky
thing
you don't notice its
appearance
until you're already in its
grasp

-*gripped*

the sun is shining
but i can't feel its warmth
i hide from its rays

a bird is singing
but i can't hear its melody
it sounds like background noise

my mom is calling
but i can't handle her words
i let it go to voicemail

my friend brought me food
but i can't taste it
it goes uneaten

i'm gulping water
but it doesn't quench my thirst
i set down the empty cup

i light a candle
but i can't smell it
i blow out the little flame

my life is moving on
but i can't see it
i close my eyes until tomorrow

-insensitive

our love story is a tree
and the last withered autumn leaf
has drifted silently to the ground
its once vibrant colors faded
beyond recognition
tarnished by disconnection

barely noticeable
this leaf and our story slip
into nonexistence
where once there was life
never to see spring again

when the world seems
too hard
to live in
take comfort
in knowing
everything is temporary
nothing is forever

even if you can't see the end
of your struggles
and your pain
right now,
you will someday

sooner than you think

change
is the only constant
in our universe

-temporary troubles

men describe the world
as they view it
through their own
two eyes
and label it Truth

even if i was
the prettiest
most interesting
sexiest
most care-free
horniest
most loving
woman on the planet
that would not
have stopped him
from lighting
his candle
in another woman's
flame

-it's not my fault

you are not
the first thought
that pops
into your head

don't be ashamed
if you don't like
the idea
your brain conjured up

we get to choose
who we are
and that begins
with our thoughts

so who you are
is defined
by your reaction
to that first thought

-you are not your thoughts

thank you
for making sure
i didn't go hungry
both when i was so excited
that i forgot to eat
and when the depression
stole my appetite

no matter how much i wish for it
no matter how warm someone is
they can't melt away my depression
i am the only one who can
claw my way out of this cave
made of ice and indifference

-cavernous responsibility

i will not blame me
it is not my fault
he is the one who wronged me

i will not blame her
it is not her fault
he is the one who wronged me

he made a commitment
to me–a trusted promise
and he broke it

men flirt with me all the time
and *every* time
i shut them down

no matter how hot they are
no matter how rich they are
no matter how strongly they come on to
me

prettier, more interesting,
more promiscuous women
will always exist, but

as much as they want us
to believe otherwise,
men have self control

when they cheat

they do so knowing
the potential consequences

the harm they cause us
the trust they're breaking
the relationship they're destroying

they hope we'll never find out
so they can have two cakes
and eat them too

they weigh the pros and cons
and decide cheating
is worth the risk

the risk of disrespecting us
the risk of gutting us
the risk of our disgust

the risk of humiliating us
the risk of angering us
the risk of our despair

they assume the risks
when they choose to act
dishonorably

-his actions, his fault

i see your invisible strength
how you go to the greatest of lengths
just to face each day
but you do it anyway
even in your darkest hour
you know the light still has power
so you trudge on with your head down
and even though you may now frown
you have hope that perhaps one day
you'll bathe in sunlight and be okay

where i once saw stars
in your eyes
now i see dust

where i once heard music
in your voice
now i hear noise

where i once saw rebirth
in your faults
now i see decay

where i once saw flowers
in your soul
now i see weeds

where i one saw rose petals
in your heart
now i see thorns

-perspective shift

the only one i owe an apology to is myself

-i'm not sorry

you are so strong
for getting out of bed
and facing the whole world
when you are not whole
when your heart has so many holes
you can't quite hold
onto all the pieces

-holding together

think of all the battles
you've won
to be standing where you are
today

your past self
would be so proud

-*victorious*

the news of your infidelity
splashed into me like cold water
simmered my mind into hatred
boiled the blood in my veins
steeped my heart in betrayal
tossed our trust in the trash

after some time i cooled
but my temperature dipped too low
sliding past sadness
until my insides were icy
my frozen body numbed me
tipped me into a depression
that filled my mind
and my cup

-iced tea infidelity

you are doing
just fine
in fact, you are doing
great

before you dismiss this
and allow
the negative thoughts
to breathe

remember
you.
are.
alive.

you
are
surviving
in this world

staying alive
is hard
but you
are doing it

surviving
is hard
but you
are doing it

in fact, you've done it
every day
you have been
on Earth

-a simple truth

open a window
and let the delicious air
of the day
sweetened by the trees
and kissed by the sun
freshen up the dark corners
of your lungs
and mind
and soul

-refresh

you matter
like the sun
matters to
the Earth

you matter
like the Earth
matters to
the moon

you matter
like the moon
matters to
the tides

you matter
like the tides
matter to
the beach

you matter
like the beach
matters to
the birds

you matter
like the birds
matter to
the trees

you matter
like the trees
matter to
the air

you matter
like the air
matters to
the sky

you matter
like the sky
matters to
the clouds

you matter
like the clouds
matter to
the rain

you matter
like the rain
matters to
the desert

–you matter

untangling

you are not alone if no one taught you how to love yourself. you are not alone if no one taught you that you are worth loving just as you are. without changing or being perfect. even if you make mistakes. you are not alone if you spent years hating yourself because they said you were the problem. you are not alone if their uncaring words planted themselves in your mind at a young age and grew along with you. you are not alone if their lies were so intertwined with your real self you could no longer tell the difference. you are not alone if their lies made you feel unworthy of love. you are not alone if their lies made it difficult to truly trust and love others sometimes.

thank you
for being my oasis
during my seasons
of drought

i am worthy
even when i don't do
everything you want me to

i am worthy
even when i don't fulfill
your every fantasy

i am worthy
even when i say
no

i am worthy
even when i put
myself first

i am worthy
whether you think
i am
or not

–i do not consent

i am allowed
to change
my mind

~~even about the big stuff~~

especially
about the big stuff

-a reminder

don't spend your energy
caring for someone
who is indifferent
to your existence

if romance is a flame,
friendship is a bed of red coals

a flame may ignite quickly
and burn brightly
but the slow and dependable
heat of the coals
always lasts longer
than the fickle flames

if you don't
positively
add
to my life
you don't
deserve
to be
in it

how much time
did i waste
being in hopeless love
with a boy or a man
who did not love me

from crushes who didn't know
i existed
to romances where i was
too persistent

love is not something you can
force
or design
or plan

-*growing pains*

stop trying
to gain the approval
of everyone
but yourself

you cannot
please everyone
so please
the only person
who matters

-approve of yourself

i don't need
to figure out
Who I Am
right now
i just need
to decide
who i am
today

-i am today

be basic. take selfies. enjoy your psl. binge that popular show. wear leggings every day. use new slang unironically. fangirl over that band. light all the candles. watch all the rom-coms. wear oversized sweaters. love that song. use a bunch of emojis. sport a messy bun every day. buy all the planners and shoes. learn how to do makeup online. like those brands. monogram everything. brunch every weekend. love rooftops. get that tiny tattoo. hang all the wall art. read romance books. stalk social media pages. drink wine and fruity cocktails. love Paris and the beach. sing into your hairbrush. wear white shoes. sport that trendy hairstyle. go to that music festival. enjoy inspirational quotes. use all the mason jars. eat the avocado toast. relax with bath bombs. overuse twinkly lights. take pictures of your food. drink iced coffee. live laugh love.

do whatever brings you happiness and stop caring about other people's irrelevant opinions.

-give yourself permission to enjoy it all

i don't owe anyone

a smile
a hug
a flawless body
a made-up face

freshly washed hair
dried hair
styled hair
hairless legs

artificially scented skin
manicured nails
tanned flesh
perfect complexion

white teeth
straight teeth
soft hands
hard tummy

modest clothes
sexy clothes
high heels on my feet
or constricted boobs

i don't owe anyone
looking like
their version

of attractive

i don't owe
anyone

my bra size
my number
my weight
my type

a conversation
a picture
a laugh
a night

a flirt
a touch
a drink
a date

a dance
a kiss
a feel
a yes—

i don't
owe
anyone
my body

foreplay
oral
sex
or my womb

i
don't
owe
anyone

a compliment
a thank you
a warm demeanor
silence

a clean house
a warm meal
a back rub
a hand job

my time
my work
my emotional labor
my skills

my ideas
my thoughts
my intelligence
my talents

my affection
my companionship
my intimacy
my love

my consent
my permission
my forgiveness
my apologies

or

an explanation

-debt free

i know you will miss me
maybe not today, but one day

the way my body
curved perfectly into yours
the beautiful things
i could do with a potato
the grand adventures
i planned for us

how my mind connected things
you could never see
how evenly matched we were
at board games
my floating voice
lulling you into slumber

the way we created our own
unique way of speaking
how my pet names for you
were often in French
the way i lit up whenever i saw
cute/beautiful/funny things

my hands caressing
every part of you

the way i made you
the center of my world

why is
my natural body
not good enough
for you

it's doing a great job
housing me

the feeling
of fighting
for things others
take for granted
is indescribable

there are so many more
ways of living
than the one
you were born into

-don't let it hold you back

our love is sunlight on skin. flowers that bloom for months. sweet spring breezes and bubbling creeks. our love is collecting seashells and chasing fireflies. windows down, radio up. dancing barefoot on the grass. our love is hotdogs hot off the backyard grill chased with grandma's apple pie. shared pizzas with toppings you don't quite like and frothy root beer floats. our love is floating on a lazy river. cookouts on sunny days. napping in a hammock and stargazing on a rooftop. our love is babies' laughter and Irish jigs. slurping watermelons. crackling campfires. our love is carving pumpkins. storytelling around the fire. building lumpy snowmen. shucking ears of sweetcorn. our love is melty s'mores and butter-drizzled popcorn. rainbow cotton candy and gooey grilled cheeses. our love is barbecue aromas, freshly cut grass, lavender fields and citrus slices. our love is litters of tiny kittens. birds chirping at first light. leaping dolphins and playful puppies. our love is dripping ice cream cones, seaside saltwater taffy, homemade lemonade and freshly baked cookies.

you didn't listen
to the songs i sent you
you didn't watch
the movies i liked
you didn't hang out
with my friends

you didn't read
my favorite books
you didn't try
my favorite foods
you didn't ask
about my hobbies

you didn't drop by
my work
you didn't care
about my passions
you didn't talk with me
about my beliefs

why did i ever think
you were interested in me

*-reflections that become clearer the
further apart we get*

why am i always
the one discovering
men's afflictions

do they really not
know
they are suffering
from depression
alcoholism
addiction
anger issues
and misogyny?

-i'm not your doctor

they said be skinny
but have curves in certain places

work out
but not too much

make your hair shiny
but not oily

wear makeup
but make it look natural

have long nails
but not too long

have tanned skin
but not too dark

look beautiful
but don't take too long getting ready

cover up
but not too much

show cleavage
but not too much

wear heels
but not too high

wear a short skirt
but then you're asking for it

let me buy you drinks
but only if you'll sleep with me

don't put out on the first date
but don't be a prude

don't sleep around
but sleep with me

be ladylike
but not in the sheets

have a threesome with me
but don't be queer

don't be stupid
but don't be smarter than me

don't be so emotional
but smile more

be sweet and innocent
but be sexy

dirty talk to me in bed
but otherwise don't swear

be a lady
but don't be like other girls

be perfectly groomed always
but don't suggest i do the same

be seen
but not heard

loosen up
but don't drink too much

don't cheat
but don't worry when i look at other
women

have a job
but don't make more than me

marry me
but not until i sample the playing field

have a job
but quit so you can have kids

have children
but not when you're too young or too old

breast feed
but never in public

be motherly
but don't nag

raise the kids
but don't let yourself go

chill out
but cook and clean the whole house

be the perfect wife
but don't expect me to be a perfect
husband

-contradictions

when it feels
like everyone
is either saying
you are not enough
or you are too much
know
that you are just enough

-my whole self is just as it should be

i do not
have
to do something
for you
just because
i'm better at it
than you

you should be
thankful
for the
practice

–develop your own skills instead of
relying on mine

not all things
that are
valuable
are
visible

-invisible not insignificant

i do not need
to anticipate
the needs
of everyone
while trampling
over my own

–choosing myself

imagine
the woman you want
to be

what does she do
how does she think
who is she

make small changes
to be more like her
every day

and one day
you'll wake up
and realize you're *her*

–small change + time = big change

thank you
for being the person
who taught me
that platonic love
is just as important
(if not more...)
as romantic love

i am
not
obligated
to do something
just because
i am
good at it

–i decide what to do with my gifts

i'm learning
how to fill
my own cup
and only give away
the overflow

and *only*
if i *want* to

would you still think
i'm beautiful

if i didn't get my nails done
if i didn't wear heels
if i didn't have soft skin
if i didn't wear perfume
if i didn't style my hair
if i didn't have any hair
if i didn't wear makeup
if i didn't hide my fat
if i didn't shave or wax
if i didn't wear bras

-now change you to i

it's so difficult
unlearning
all the harmful stuff
that has been baked
into you
since you were a bun
in the oven

but ripping yourself apart
is so worth it
when you discover
you're not a bun
you're a cupcake

-unbaking

be the version
of yourself
that *you* love

not the one
your mom loves
or your grandma loves
or your boyfriend loves
or your friend loves
or your teacher loves
or your boss loves
or society loves

you.

you are worthy of so much more than
being disregarded or invalidated by the
one who is supposed to be your partner.
you are worthy of so much more than
being lied to and manipulated. you are
worthy of so much more than being
unsupported. you are worthy of so much
more than insults from the one who is
supposed to love you the most. you are
worthy of so much more than sacrificing
your dreams and aspirations for someone
else's. you are worthy of so much more
than taking care of everyone when no one
is taking care of you. you are worthy of so
much more than being taken for granted.
you are worthy of so much more than
settling for someone who doesn't
prioritize you.

i spend 86,400
seconds a day
with myself

i am the only one
who will ever truly
know myself

if i give unconditional love
to anyone
it should be me

people keep asking
if i'm seeing anyone new
as if dating a man
is the only way
for me to be happy

as if i'm not doing
anything
with my life
if i'm not dating a man

as if i'm not ~~doing~~
anything
~~with my life~~
if i'm not dating a man

*-i am more than my relationship
status*

why do we address women
by their marital status
but men are all just mr.

they act like there is a *before*
and *after* marriage
for women only

like marriage
is the single most important goal
in any woman's life

so much so
they name us accordingly
miss and mrs.

and by naming us this way
they *define* us
by our marital status

single or married
anything in between doesn't count
anything else doesn't matter

your relationship
isn't legitimate
until you're married

you
aren't legitimate

until you're married

if you're a woman

-ms.

thank you
for showing me
who you really are
before i built
my whole life
on your land

that way
i only had to mourn
a garden
instead of
a forest

why are men
viewed as main characters
and women are only viewed
through their inverse relations
to men

men are strong
so women must be weak

men are smart
so women must be stupid

men are analytical
so women must be emotional

men don't care
so women must do all the caring

men have penises
so women must receive them

men are the stars
so women must be the supporting roles

-women and men are not opposites

you deserve to be seen. you deserve to be heard. you deserve to be understood. you deserve to be loved.

women
climax
twice as fast
without
a partner

    -*self-*~~*sufficient*~~ *efficient*

being your authentic self
means disappointing people
for not fulfilling their fantasy
of who they think you are

but they are not
the author
of your story

they are not
the main character
of your story

you are.

and if they
only support
their fictional idea
of you

it is okay
if their chapter
in your story
comes to a close

–write your own fairytale

don't be so
terrified
to say something
wrong
that you never
say
anything

write the message
leave the comment
dial the number
make the art

-share without fear

i'll make it official:
my relationship status
doesn't indicate
my worth
or my happiness

the timing was wrong before
now the timing's wrong again
now we'll spend
the early mornings and late nights
of our lives
wondering what if
hoping the universe
might bring us together again
i've heard the third time
is the charm
what if it's ours

-twilight

the world
is messy
and that is okay

i
am messy
and that is okay

everything doesn't have
a clear and perfect definition
and that is okay

i don't have
a clear and perfect definition
and that is okay

not everything fits
in neat little boxes
and that is okay

i don't fit
in neat little boxes
and that is okay

-messy doesn't equal bad

i vow
to stop saying
i'm sorry
to the world
and start saying
i'm sorry
to myself

my worth
does not
come from
my proximity
to a man

i am not
somebody's girlfriend
somebody's daughter
somebody's secretary
somebody's mom
somebody's mistress
somebody's granddaughter
somebody's housekeeper
somebody's niece
somebody's fiancée
somebody's assistant
somebody's aunt
somebody's nurse
somebody's wife

i am
somebody

-a woman is somebody

i admit
i am bitter
but if you sampled
me
that's not
the only flavor
you'd taste

sweet and spicy
salty and tangy
sour yet rich
delicious
unique
complexity

-bitter like fine wine

you deserve to have people who accept
you exactly as you are. who want you to
be no less than your unique, messy,
imperfect, whole self. who celebrate the
growth and changes you undergo with
you. people who help you to stretch out
and take up space. who encourage you to
follow every dream you have. who give
just as freely as they take.

you don't need to be happy
all the time

you don't need to be grateful
all the time

you don't need to be positive
all the time

"negative" emotions are healthy
and necessary

even sadness
jealousy
and anger

acknowledge your emotions
all of them
accept them
process them

balance is key

-*emotional tightrope*

tying

the world needs you
and you need the world

like flowers need bees
and bees need flowers

like trees need birds
and birds need trees

like oceans need fish
and fish need oceans

the world needs you
and you need the world

-mutual

i choose to love myself
because even if i never earn
the love of another
or even if another's love
fades after a while
and we drift apart
i never have to worry
about earning my own love
my self-love fading in time
or being without my own company

-i am the one

my head is so full
of big dreams
i sometimes forget
that little dreams
are magical too

–dream little

would you have loved me if
i had already learned my self worth

-i already know the answer

you asked another girl to the dance
and then danced with me all night

you wanted me
but not enough to say it loudly

i deserve someone
who will scream my name from rooftops

you wanted me
but hesitated to pick me in front of
everyone

i deserve to be someone's
first choice

-i deserve bold

you're a strong river
providing water
to whoever needs it
never asking for anything in return

but if you aren't careful
you'll give away
every last drop
of yourself

and when you run dry
no one will be there
to replenish
your waters

so only give freely
to those who'll bring
spring rains & summer showers
autumn mists & winter snowfalls

because you deserve
your banks and shores
to be
overflowing

peace
might be
the greatest
gift
you can ever
give
yourself

-choosing peace

why can't i
exist

in public
in a store
in the gym
in a train

online
on social media
on the phone
on a video call

at work
at school
at the doctor
at home

in a car
on a sidewalk
at a family function
or anywhere

without men assuming
i belong in their beds

-treat me like a whole human

the female experience
is just as universal
as the male experience

-*50% of the world*

my value
is not tied to
my ability to bear children
or serve men

i am valuable
all on my own

-inherently valuable

would he love me if i stopped
cutting my hair
coloring my hair
styling my hair

would he love me if i stopped
shaving my legs
my armpits
my pubes

would he love me if i stopped
waxing my eyebrows
plucking my nipple hairs
bleaching my mustache

would he love me in my natural body?

if the answer is no, he never loved me at
all

he only loved the body i labored over
to transform into his version of attractive

-hairy predicament

people will fight
so hard
to keep believing
the hypocritical
oppressive
nonsensical
beliefs
that society
invisibly forced
upon them

the world
had me thinking
i was only
a grain of sand

turns out,
i'm a pearl

-*precious*

my worth is not derived
from my youth
or my beauty
or my chastity
or how sexy men think i am

i want to be like most other women
most women i know
are kind and thoughtful
smart and resilient
strong and compassionate
brave and creative
good and peaceful

most women i know
do so much
with so little
and work so hard
with so little gratitude
and give so much
for so little in return

most women i know
do what needs doing
even if no one sees them do it

most women i know
keep the world spinning
even if no one helps them do it

> -*"you aren't like most girls" is not a
> compliment*

most men
will never
ever deserve
your beautiful
meticulous
caring
labor

or your precious
time

or your incredible
body

or your selfless
love

−you deserve more than they
will give

hundreds of countries
thousands of languages
millions of cities
countless cultures and religions

and yet you think
there is one
right way
to be a woman

are you
sure.
about.
that.

-are you sure about that

women are oceans
and lakes
and ponds

they give up their water
so the rain
can share it
with everyone

the oceans and lakes and ponds
don't dry up
as long as the borrowed water
finds its way back to them

but what happens
when men collect the rain
and don't return it

pretty soon
it stops raining
at all

-water cycle

hateful men
deserve the loneliness
they have brought upon themselves

*-if they want my affection, they
need to treat me well*

as much as i want it
long for it
crave it
i don't need
someone to be
in love with me
but i do need
to be in love
with myself

sisters and mothers
i see you

i see the men
have gouged out their own eyes
afraid to behold your whole selves

maybe they are right to be afraid
you make the world run
with a mere fraction
of their resources

you carry everyone on your back
children and husbands
aging parents and friends
no one left behind

you are stronger
than they've ever been

-caring is strength

sometimes i wish i could choose
to be romantically interested
in women

-a secret thought

you don't need
to blend in
with the pitch black
of the night sky
or camouflage yourself
as a blade of grass
in a sprawling lawn

flowers and sunsets
waterfalls and stars
things that stand out
are often the most beautiful

i believe the same is true
for people
someone being
their most authentic
weird silly colorful
whole self
is a masterpiece
it just feels right

-don't be afraid to stand out

i deserve
to have my voice heard
among
singers and prophets
authors and politicians
scientists and preachers
and loud men

-*voices*

i don't need men
to approve of me

i don't need to behave
in certain ways
in order to gain male approval
i just need to be myself
and i will attract the men
who will accept me
appreciate me
and adore me
as i am

-*authentic attraction*

whatever you are dying to do
do it now

don't wait
for a better time
for more money
for someone else
for anything

tomorrow is not a guarantee
everything changes
usually in ways you'd never suspect

things i knew for certain
ten, five, or even one year ago
exist no longer
except in my memory

health declines
wars are declared
energy wanes
pandemics happen
money is spent
recessions come
relationships end
natural disasters strike
time stops short

no one knows
what tomorrow holds

so take the risk
while you still have the chance

you will regret
the things you didn't do
far more
than the things you did

eat the food
take the trip
go to the party
move to that place
visit the person
try the activity
attend the event
buy the tickets
get a new job
wear the dress
go on the adventure

i beg you

   -*live your dreams out loud right
   now*

you are the hero
of your story
not your dad
or your boyfriend
or your husband
or your child
YOU

-saving yourself

I
am the love
of my life

-repeat it until it sticks

ask yourself
will it matter
one year from now?

if the answer is no
just let it go

-inconsequential

why did we take
so many
multiple choice tests
in school

in real life
the answer
is not one
out of four

it's the one
you didn't know
you were
searching for

-blindsided

the universe heard me
i asked for love
and you came to me
what took you so long?

-patience paid off

you touch my heart
in ways i didn't know
were possible
in places i didn't know
existed
in times i didn't know
i needed you

-unexpected

love is the relentless ocean tide
ever ebbing and flowing
pulling our hearts together
just as it's tethered to the moon
its waves crashing against
the shore of our souls
etching our names
in the sands of time
leaving behind imprints
that cannot be erased

sleeping next to you
i sometimes forget
that i'm not dreaming
because now that i'm with you
my dreams
have become my reality

-sometimes dreams come true

when we embrace
i want to lean into you
the way a river
leans into the earth
and leaves the earth forever changed
with its impression

the river carves
its name
into the land
engraving their story
so deeply
it will remain even
if the river changes course

i hope i touch you
so deeply
our story lives on in your
skin and heart and soul
even if one day
we part ways
or change course

-canyon

i didn't find love
until i stopped
looking for a partner
and started looking
for myself

they lied to us
told us love
was something that happened to you
perhaps accidentally

but we had to learn
the hard way
that real love
is something you *make* happen

a conscious choice
that you have to make
over and over again
each and every day

-choosing to fall in love

you deserve someone
who doesn't just give
in the ways
that are easy for them
that they're good at already
that they enjoy the most

you deserve someone
who gives
in the ways
that you need
that you want
even if it is difficult for them
even if they have to learn how
even if they don't enjoy it

because wouldn't you do the same
for them

-*needs over inconvenience*

if i give up my last name
for yours
what are you giving up
for me?

*-love is a compromise, not a
sacrifice*

our love is a limitless voyage
across a boundless sea
of possibilities
our hearts the vessels
navigating the unpredictable
waves of life
the fluttering sails of our souls guided
by the glittering constellations
of our shared dreams

it is so much easier
to love
you
than it is to love
myself

for some reason
i look past your
flaws
and fixate
on my own

you make mistakes
and i easily forgive you
why can't i grant
the same grace
to myself

-self-love is hard

you deserve a kisses you goodbye every morning love. a gentle love. an empathetic love. a cooks just as often as you love. a hides you love notes love. a buys the perfect gift because they know you so well and really put in the effort to get it right love. an intentional love. a keeps a to do list of their half of the chores love. a slow dancing in the living room love. a cuddling on the couch after work love. a texts you because something reminded them of you love. a makes you climax every time love. a considerate love.

having children
is not the only way
for a woman to be fulfilled

i made a home
in your warmth
and it protects me
from the relentless cold
of this world

-you're my cozy cottage

love isn't
when he pays for dinner

love is
when he secretly rehearses a song in the
cold garage for a month to serenade you
with

love isn't
when he holds the door open for you

love is
when he finds the nearest store to buy
you socks when your new shoes start
giving you blisters

love isn't
when he buys you candy hearts and
random flowers on Valentine's Day

love is
when he buys you your favorite candy
and your favorite flowers on a random
Tuesday–just because

love isn't
when he makes you dinner one time

love is

when he splits cooking and chores with
you 50/50 all the time

love isn't
when he buys you diamonds

love is
when he brings you vegan cupcakes when
you have PMS and said you're craving
them

love isn't
when he gets down on one knee

love is
when he takes off work to take care of
you when you're sick

love isn't
when he tries to prove his love to you

love is
when he genuinely cares for you and
would make sacrifices for your happiness,
even if you never knew about them

-love isn't what we were told

153

you deserve to be loved
like you're the only woman
on earth

-cherishable

a true partner
whose love is genuine
will not only consider
your needs
(and desires)
but anticipate
them

you will
find a love
who treats you
like the galaxy
you are

i will love you
until the sequoia trees
are so fat with age
you could hide
a mountain behind them

i hope you get everything
you truly desire
not the things you put on a wish list
the things your heart burns for
whatever will wholly satiate
your deepest longings
ardently fulfill
your greatest yearnings
profoundly satisfy
your bottomless hungers
and forever fuel your soul

-my hope for you

when we planted our roots
side by side
we couldn't know
if we would thrive

the climate turned harsh
from temperate to desert
but we evolved to embrace
the dry dirt

through winds and storms
and floods and drought
we found out what changing
was all about

altered in size
and color and shape
our insides, too
weren't the same

while our roots grew deeper
and thicker and longer
our trunks intertwined
and made us stronger

instead of chasing
after the sun
i choose to stay here
curled up next to this one

-entangled

to not do list #1:

- shrink myself
- try to force someone to love me
- stay with someone who doesn't listen to or consider me
- take my friends for granted
- let heartbreak consume my every waking moment
- let my inner critic put down my natural body
- question my self worth
- give everything to people who give me the minimum
- believe the bullshit society has told me about women, myself included
- apologize when i'm not in the wrong
- stay quiet
- conform to someone else's idea of "beauty"
- let anyone or anything keep me from loving myself 100%
- wait to live the life i want
- settle for less than i deserve
- live my life for anyone but myself
- forget that i am the love of my life

my love
isn't
unconditional

except
when it's self-love

-love yourself unconditionally

have you claimed your free self-love workbook yet?

ignite the life-changing flames of self-love within you, dear soul!

step into a realm **where love for yourself flourishes**. join our vibrant community today and receive celina maeve's exclusive 2-week self-love workbook that will **transform your relationship with yourself**. immerse yourself in heartfelt prompts and empowering exercises...this transformative gift will **guide you on a journey of self-discovery and unapologetic self-acceptance**. this is your moment to prioritize yourself and **unlock the boundless power of self-love**. claim your free workbook now and let celina maeve's compassionate words be your guiding light as you nourish your soul.

your path to profound self-love begins here.

claim your free, exclusive 2-week self-love workbook at:

celinamaeve.com

about the author

hey there, lovely soul!

i'm celina maeve, a self-love poet, and i'm thrilled you've discovered my poetry book. my passion lies in spreading the message of self-love, helping others feel less alone, and fostering deep love and appreciation for themselves. mental health, love and relationships, feminism, body positivity, and equality are all subjects close to my heart, and I use my voice to amplify them. when I'm not writing, I find solace in snuggling with cats, savoring tea, singing, and exploring Asian food spots. nature also brings me peace. thank you for getting to know me better—i hope my writing inspires and uplifts you on your journey of self-love and discovery.

celina maeve

connect with me here:

celinamaevepoetry

celinamaeve.com

exclusive
preview

unveil the raw power of self-love and body positivity in this exclusive preview of my next book, "scrapbook of my skin," where love poems intertwine with feminist ideas to create a captivating tapestry of empower-ment. prepare to be moved, inspired, and awakened as you delve into these powerful words...

find out more here:

celinamaeve.com/soms

my scars and calluses
stretch marks and wrinkles
are tiny glimpses
of my life's story
like stickers on a car bumper
or photos in the scrapbook
of my skin
each one marking
places and experiences
full of memories
of my unique narrative
that i will cherish
as proof
my story existed

-*scrapbook of my skin*

celinamaeve.com/soms

do not
let the world convince you
that your 100% natural body
is not *stunningly* beautiful

you are perfect
as you are

     -au naturel

----

i am so powerful
and my body is so powerful

my skin heals itself
when it is cut

i heal myself
when i am wounded

i possess the powers
of regeneration
of healing
of growth

and not just in my skin

celinamaeve.com/soms

i fell so hard for you
it took me a long time
to stand up and realize
i was never in love
with the real you—
i was only in love
with my fictional version
of you

no wonder why
i thought you were perfect
i dreamt up my perfect partner
and glued it
onto your skin

----

i'm done
with shrinking myself
to fit into the cookie cutter
that is a man's idea
of what a woman
should be

-i am not made of cookie dough

celinamaeve.com/soms

i never want to hear
"you haven't aged a day"

each day
i get to feel
the warmth of the sun
on my skin
is the most precious
gift

i want to wear
my wrinkles
and bronze age spots
and silver hair
like gold medals
earned for surviving
another year
or decade

-medals of maturity

----

valuing your body's needs
over people's opinions
is the greatest act
of self love

celinamaeve.com/soms

Printed in Great Britain
by Amazon

28983025R00096